DAPHNE du MAURIER COUNTRY

Martyn Shallcross

BOSSINEY BOOKS

To Bernice
who introduced me to the world of
Daphne du Maurier – with love

First published in 1987 by
Bossiney Books
St Teath, Bodmin, Cornwall.

Typeset and Printed by
Clowes Book Printers
St Columb, Cornwall.

ISBN 0 948158 36 0

PLATE ACKNOWLEDGMENTS
Front Cover: By Ken Duxbury.
Ray Bishop: pages 7, 11, 13, 17, 24, 25, 38, 39, 42/3, 48, 50, 51, 63, 64, 65, 66/7, 74, 75, 80, 81, 89, 90, 94, 98, 99, 102, 104/5, 107. 111 and back cover.
David Clarke: pages 32, 34, 35, 52, 60/1, 62, 72, 73, 79, 82.
Ken Duxbury: pages 16, 19, 20.
George Ellis: pages 29, 87, 92.
Felicity Young: pages 23, 37.
Alice Boyd: page 88
Marylou North: pages 40/41
All other photographs from the Author's collection.
Front Cover: Lantic Bay near Polruan.
Back Cover: Fowey Harbour and Dame Daphne du Maurier.

Acknowledgment
I would like to express my heartfelt thanks to Dame Daphne du Maurier for her help over the years and for opening her private world to me: also to her family especially Christian Browning, her son, and to members of her household at Kilmarth who always give me a warm welcome. I would also like to acknowledge the help of Victor Spinetti, Stewart Granger, the late James Mason, Lady Fitzwilliam, Tamsin Olivier, Joan Fontaine, Donald Sutherland, Val Jones, Barbara Mart, Margaret Fellows and Mavis and Bill Stubbs. Also my mother Essie who first showed me some of Daphne du Maurier Country.

MARTYN SHALLCROSS

Contents

About the Author and the Book

Daphne du Maurier Country is a very special look at Cornwall in that the internationally-famous novelist has set important stories here. Many of her novels and short stories are steeped in Cornish history and romance. Words and photographs, many of them especially commissioned for this publication, explore locations which fired Dame Daphne's imagination in such memorable story-telling as *Rebecca, The King's General, Jamaica Inn* and others.

This, Bossiney's one-hundred-and-fifty-second title is a treasure chest for those who love Cornwall and for all people who have read the du Maurier novels in scores of languages across the world.

Of her beloved Cornwall, Dame Daphne says with feeling: 'The beauty and the mystery beckon still.'

Martyn Shallcross was born in Stratford on Avon, brought up in Warwickshire and educated in Staffordshire where he obtained a degree in history and qualifications as a teacher. He began in show business at college where he worked on the book *Love Scene* by Jesse Lasky, Jr and Pat Silver about the lives of Laurence Olivier and Vivien Leigh.

He met Daphne du Maurier in the late 1960s in Crete and corresponded with her during the early 70s when she helped him with the book on Olivier and Leigh. Dame Daphne also introduced him to Joan Fontaine and, as a result, he arranged *The Guardian* lecture in which he was the interviewer at the National Film Theatre.

Martyn Shallcross later worked for Barry Norman in BBC television on programmes like *Film 87* and the *Hollywood Greats* series of programmes. As a freelance film journalist he has interviewed some of the most famous actors and actresses in the world: people like Ingrid Bergman and Charlton Heston, Bette Davis and James Mason, Marlene Dietrich and Stewart Granger, Sophia Loren and Elizabeth Taylor.

RIGHT: **Daphne du Maurier photographed with Martyn Shallcross at Kilmarth in 1983. Kilmarth has been her home since 1967.**

Daphne du Maurier Country

It is a remarkable fact that three of the most popular novelists in this century have set important stories here in Cornwall.

Dame Daphne du Maurier, Winston Graham and Howard Spring are just three distinguished authors who have built international reputations with works steeped in Cornish history and romance. Moreover, this is an ongoing Cornish tradition in that today E.V. Thompson and Janice Elliott continue to live and work here.

Cornwall, then, over the years has triggered creativity. As with the case of so many eminent painters in Cornwall, none of these writers is Cornish born. Like so many men and women in the arts, they have been drawn to Cornwall, lured by the atmosphere and the contrasting beauty of the place — and the places.

Denys Val Baker in his book *The Timeless Land, The Creative Spirit in Cornwall,* has touched very specifically on the subject of Dame Daphne's relationship with Cornwall – and how she turned that relationship into memorable work.

'Who, for instance, driving over Bodmin Moor and suddenly coming upon the forlorn outline of the now famous Jamaica Inn, at Bolventor, can fail to feel the impact of such a stark, bleak, and out-of-this-world setting? How well, in turn, did Daphne du Maurier capitalise upon this atmosphere in her bestseller *Jamaica Inn,* deepening the shadows, stressing the unease, heightening the general impression of eeriness, of other-worldliness.'

RIGHT: **The coast below the fields of Menabilly Barton – with Gribbin Head on the right.**

Joan Fontaine as Dona St Columb in the film of 'Frenchman's Creek'. 'The places that have inspired Daphne du Maurier are often equally as beautiful as many of her written passages.'

How many people, I wonder, realise Daphne du Maurier is alive and well and still residing in her beloved Cornwall?

Here we look at her Cornish career and immediately we discover there is something extraordinary in her ability to create stories — one novel *Rebecca* having grown into a publishing legend in that it appeals to thousands of readers all over the world wherever books are read.

The passage of time is often swift and one's memory of the past can often be overlooked and forgotten. People may change and the memories of a previous generation alter, but somehow the memory of a certain period or epoch can remain unchanged in one's mind forever. The cause may be a certain event, a dash of colour, a line of dialogue, a shadow, a sigh, a smile, a memory. To create an illusion and an image these memories should be set aside in one's mind and kept as a wonderful reminder of a golden age.

What makes one person special and able to evoke love and affection for a certain film or novel is a difficult question to answer; maybe a certain way of smiling or an interesting lilt of the voice during some spoken dialogue. If you place these all together they produce some sort of magical essence that one remembers over the years. Everyone is special, but perhaps some are more gifted either with original and rare beauty or incomparable intellect. For anyone, therefore, to create this affection and love from just a few novels is in itself something special.

In the minds of many people Daphne du Maurier and Cornwall are what Thomas Hardy is to Dorset and the Brontë sisters are to Yorkshire. She will always be associated with the essential romance and adventure of Cornwall. Cornwall, over the years, has provided Daphne with the background for many of her most successful novels: *Jamaica Inn, The Loving Spirit, Frenchman's Creek, My Cousin Rachel, The House on the*

RIGHT: The River Fowey in its early stages, photographed by Ray Bishop, in the Fowey Valley below Bolventor and Jamaica Inn, the setting for Daphne du Maurier's famous novel. This river has played a big part in the history and legends of Cornwall. Some say King Doniert died, through drowning, when the Fowey flooded. That early King of Cornwall's burial stone stands nearby on the higher ground – on the road to Minions.

Strand, Rebecca and *The King's General.* Many Cornish places have been immortalised – her descriptive narrative making them even more famous.

The *true* location for some of the scenes in her novels are unknown to the great majority of her readers. The private world of Daphne du Maurier has remained secret for many years, the door always locked to outsiders: yet the places that have inspired her are often equally as beautiful as many of her written passages.

For almost half a century Daphne du Maurier has entertained us about life and living in her imaginary world. Like the Brontë sisters of Yorkshire, most of her ideas have come from within her own vivid imagination. Her decriptive narrative and sheer readability and the success of her books have all widened Cornwall's fame or notoriety.

Now, in her eightieth year, she continues to live in the same Dower House near Fowey, taking walks on the nearby beach with her beloved Scottish terrier dogs. Gone are the hectic days when she was producing one bestseller after another. This, then, is perhaps the moment to take a long affectionate look at the writer and her relationship with Cornwall.

MARTYN SHALLCROSS 1987

RIGHT: **Fowey which has played such an important part in the life and work of Daphne du Maurier. The novels of Sir Arthur Quiller-Couch made it a popular place for Edwardian visitors. It is a quaint town, steeped in history, ancient and modern, and cannot be neatly, easily described. Sarah Foot, in her book 'Fowey: River and Town', touched on the enigma when she wrote: 'It is difficult to describe the real essence of Fowey Town. Whether you enter it through the hilly streets which wend their way down to the river, or whether you arrive on the Bodinnick car ferry and see the town laid out before you from the midst of the river, it is always a compelling, enchanted place.**

'And I think it is true to say that although outsiders may come and appreciate the beauties of Fowey Town, there is something secret, guarded by its inhabitants, that can only be truly known and appreciated by them.'

Why Cornwall?

The question is inevitable, for Cornwall is different and for many a foreign land.

Maybe it is a combination of things: a long Cornish history and people with a language of their own, ancient customs, superstition and legends. They all combine to create a uniqueness.

Daphne has immortalised Cornwall in her fiction and she has been fortunate in that a high percentage of her work has been transferred to the screen and turned into outstanding film.

In the context of the du Maurier family we know that, like many other city families, they came to Cornwall for holidays. The beautiful beaches, the coastline and the recreational activities: all these would have been factors in the fascination experienced by the young Daphne du Maurier and her family when they first visited Cornwall over half a century ago. Daphne, in particular, began to discover the area around Fowey and its magic drew her back again and again. The picturesque harbour especially, with its ships going about their daily business, appealed to her, and the stories of the local people appealed to the writer in her nature, for such stories were to lie dormant in her subconscious and later fire her imagination.

Cornwall has attracted the Bohemian like a magnet and this, too, could have been a factor as Daphne, the daughter of actor-manager Sir Gerald du Maurier and the grand-daughter of George du Maurier,

RIGHT: **It was at Ferryside across the river from Fowey that the young Daphne wrote her novel 'The Loving Spirit'.**

Today at Ferryside (above), now the home of Miss Angela du Maurier, photographed right in 1979, stands the great figurehead of a sunken ship. It has considerable significance in the life and times of Dame Daphne. It was at Pont Pill that the young Daphne du Maurier had boated around this ancient figurehead – later given to her – and it was this figurehead which became the inspiration for her first book 'The Loving Spirit'.

Something of the magic of Ferryside was captured by Angela du Maurier in her chapter in 'My Cornwall', one of Bossiney's first publications in 1973: '. . . to sit by a coal fire in winter evenings in a room hewn from rock listening to the water lapping outside over the slip, the same slip where I sit on summer evenings watching gulls and kingfishers. To draw my curtains in the morning and to look at the beauty of Fowey harbour from my bedside, a view which never ceases to give joy. Cornwall is a county of magic. And my bit of Cornwall is the village of Bodinnick, a small slice of that magic, where a one-time boatyard is my haven.'

famous for *Trilby,* was exposed from an early age to writers, actors and creative personalities. Jesse Lasky, Jr, son of the famous film pioneer, remembers one visit to the du Mauriers at Cannon Hall in Hampstead: 'In those days, before her marriage, Daphne was a real Bohemian, reading poetry and acting rather unconventionally.'

We can imagine the contrast between the sophistication and excitement of social Hampstead and the tranquil pleasures of Fowey.

The du Mauriers usually rented houses, but the house which especially won their hearts was a Swiss-type cottage near the ferry at Bodinnick. After renting it for a period the family bought Ferryside, and it was here that Daphne began her very first novel *The Loving Spirit.* The story was to revolve around the village of Plyn. This was actually Polruan and the boat building family originated from the boatyard also in Polruan. Gazing across the harbour Daphne was captivated by the view— all of which helped her to conceive the story of the fictional family. She used local places and, in turn, her narrative described and immortalised the area around Fowey.

From the windows of Ferryside Daphne was to have her first sight of her future husband. After that initial meeting a courtship developed, and they were soon married. Like the young couple in *The Loving Spirit,* they went by boat to Lanteglos Church for their wedding. Daphne told me: 'All I did on my honeymoon was to go up the Helford River to Frenchman's Creek.'

We find this curious intermingling of fact and fiction running through Dame Daphne's life. *The Birds,* for example, so successful as a film for the big screen, directed by the legendary Hitchcock, really owed its genesis to Cornwall: 'I got the idea for the story of *The Birds* from watching the farmer plough the fields behind the farm at Menabilly Barton, and the seagulls chased the tractor, flying and darting down, trying apparently to attack the farmer. This is how I got the idea of birds attacking people.'

RIGHT: **Polruan always fascinated Daphne right from an early age. It was the inspiration for the village of Plyn in 'The Loving Spirit'.**

Historically and emotionally Daphne has found great fascination in the Brontë family, but that surely came later. If we are to find the real genesis of her love affair with Cornwall, then we have to go back to childhood: to the five-year-old little girl who came to Mullion Cove on the Lizard Peninsula, and five years later the same but different girl on Kennack Sands, also on the Lizard Peninsula.

The Brontë sisters may have been born and brought up in Yorkshire, but they had a Cornish mother, Maria Branwell, who came from Penzance. Their novels became literary landmarks: *Jane Eyre* and *Wuthering Heights.* To what extent Daphne's writing style has been influenced by the Brontë sisters is open to debate. What we can say for certain is that her first novel, *The Loving Spirit,* was inspired in title alone from a haunting poem written by Emily Brontë. There is a further parallel in that both sisters, like Daphne du Maurier merged personal experience and imagination and became closely associated with an area. In their case, they are identified with the towns and moors of Yorkshire. It is interesting to note too that Daphne's association with Cornwall is highlighted in her book *Vanishing Cornwall.* One might almost call it a Cornish autobiography — and in it she devotes a whole chapter to the Brontë family and their Cornish connections.

It was in 1960 that Daphne du Maurier's *The Infernal World of Branwell Brontë,* appeared, published by Victor Gollancz. In it she turned her literary and historical searchlights on to this short-lived but highly talented family of Haworth Parsonage. Manuscripts, running to many hundreds of thousands of words, were penned inside its four walls.

Branwell Brontë's work may not have had quite the same polish and power of his famous sisters, but his was a boyhood and youth of staggering productivity. His flame flickered early — brilliantly — so much so that the lives and loves of his imaginary characters was a burning out process and, by the age of twenty-one, his invention was exhausted. He died on a Sunday morning in 1848, aged only thirty-one.

LEFT: **Sitting one day on the terrace at the Fowey Hotel, Daphne pointed out landmarks to me. 'It was a shipbuilding yard over there at Polruan that was my inspiration for part of the story in "The Loving Spirit".'**

Branwell's was indeed an 'infernal world', 'haunted by demons' seeing 'luminous substances in his imagination' and suffering 'frequent trembling of the limbs'.

His biographer took the view that he was more likely to have been suffering from fits rather than delirium tremens, a condition triggered by alcohol. Her writing and careful research portray a sad figure — ultimately unloved in a contented household: a curious castaway. At the very outset of the book, there are lines quoted from William Cowper's *The Castaway.*

In one of my meetings with Daphne she told me, 'I nearly drank some laudanum like Branwell, but I gave up and poured it down the sink.'

Cornwall's past has been beautifully recalled in many of the books of Daphne du Maurier. The historical novel is perhaps one of the most difficult types of writing. There is a certain limiting effect, there is the need to adhere to a particular pattern — a pattern defined by history which demands a marked degree of accuracy. 'It's a difficult business,' she once admitted. 'The fact is I've always been interested in the past. The real problem is striking a balance. You've lots of truth to go on, and yet you want to hold the attention of your reader. You play about with things a bit, but it's a little tricky . . . you hate to go wrong with basic history. The older I get, the keener I get on truth. Naturally though I take liberties with dialogue . . . the historical novelist must.'

Getting back to the inevitable 'Why Cornwall?', when asked that question today, Dame Daphne replies: 'It is still so lovely even in the rain, I would rather be out walking on the beach and headland and looking out at my Cornwall, than anything else I come to think of.' Even at the age of eighty the magic of Cornwall still holds a spell over her.

RIGHT: Branwell Brontë, drawn by Felicity Young. A character who clearly intrigued Daphne du Maurier, whose life was truly an 'infernal world' as the title of her biography announced.

As Sir John Betjeman reflected, Fowey 'is a haunted town made for sailors and pedestrians'. John Rashleigh's ship the 'Francis of Fowey' sailed with Drake against the Spanish Armada. Legend has it that Jesus, as a boy, came ashore at Punche's Cross with his uncle Joseph of Arimathea on a tin trading excursion. Foy Quiller-Couch, who lived at The Haven remembers the American ships leaving Fowey for the D Day landings: '. . . just a great black mass, for no lights could be used.' The seagoing tradition is a strong one. In 1347 Fowey sent as many as 47 ships to Edward III's siege of Calais – Fowey was then the most important port of the south coast. In 1457 the French invaded the town.

The Versatile du Maurier

It was in 1934 that she really broke into the headlines with a biography of her father Sir Gerald du Maurier. The candour of that biography apparently upset some people, but Sir Gerald's daughter had no regrets: 'Father always said, "You've got to tell the truth," and I wrote the book as he would have written it . . . at least, that's how I see it.'

Despite her theatre background, the young Daphne had no desire to go on the stage: 'I enjoyed watching my father act. I thought him wonderful, but the theatre didn't appeal to me personally. In fact, going backstage after a show, when people came round with their congratulations, I found it all most embarrassing.'

Daphne did, of course, write for the theatre — *The Years Between, September Tide* and an adaptation of her bestselling *Rebecca.*

The range of du Maurier authorship is very extensive. It includes one volume of autobiography, *Growing Pains;* five biographies, a baker's dozen of novels, five volumes of short stories, one travel publication *Vanishing Cornwall,* two plays and then in 1981 *The Rebecca Notebook and Other Memories.* This last book fascinatingly reveals how *Rebecca* came to be written: its origin and development. The memories section is partly autobiographical and to some extent about her beliefs. Readers also encounter her distinguished grandfather George du Maurier, whose *Punch* illustrations made him a famous figure; and her father Gerald, for whom Sir James Barrie wrote *Peter Pan.* Her writing in this section also ranges across such subjects as romantic love and widowhood, religion and success — and death.

Today when there are no new du Maurier novels, it is perhaps not easy for a younger generation to understand that in her heyday Dame Daphne won golden opinions from all over the world. *Time and Tide*

A rare photograph of Dame Daphne reading one of her own books.

reviewing her novel *The Scapegoat* first published by Gollancz in 1957 wrote: 'From the original beginning to the inevitable end this book is one of her best.'

Here is Ronald Bryden writing in *The Spectator* in April 1962: 'Penguin Books have recognised by giving her the full regal reprinting previously awarded Lawrence, Graham Greene and Evelyn Waugh, that Miss du Maurier is one of the world's great literary phenomena. It is about time somebody did. Miss du Maurier's novels have been read by millions of people in scores of languages. The films made from them have been seen by millions more. In France, her works rank with Durrell's and Charles Morgan's, in the U.S. they are automatic book-club choices. Largely by her efforts, Britain still leads the world in romantic fiction.'

However an *Observer* critic reviewing *The Birds* said: 'Anyone starting this book under the impression that he may sleepily relax is in for a shock . . . continually provokes both pity and terror.' Such words completely demolish the idea that she was purely and simply a romantic novelist.

Critics on the other side of the Atlantic invariably gave Daphne a good press, *The New York Times* once referring to her as 'in a class by herself', and *McCall's* called her 'a master of suspense' while *Chicago Tribune Book World* said: 'Daphne du Maurier sweeps dust away and brings her stories alive. It is a rare talent . . . In this century few English-speaking authors seem to keep that particular magic. Somerset Maugham was one, and du Maurier is most definitely another.'

RIGHT: A portrait of Lady du Maurier, mother of Daphne, Angela and Jeanne, a painter who lives on Dartmoor, across the Tamar in Devon. This photograph, taken at home, at Ferryside, on 5 August 1946, is by George Ellis of Bodmin.

Jamaica Inn

Jamaica Inn was first published in January 1936. In those days it was a temperance house on the twisting, turning moorland road linking Bodmin and Launceston. But in her imagination Daphne du Maurier saw it in the 1700s. Although genuine place names figure in the pages, in her note at the beginning of the novel the author says, 'Characters and events described are entirely imaginary.'

The heroine is recently-orphaned Mary Yelland who leaves her home at idyllic Helford to go and live with her aunt at Jamaica Inn, Bolventor. Mary is horrified to find that her once pretty Aunt Patience has become a shadow of herself — living under the influence of her husband Joss Merlyn, a bully of a man who is engaged in smuggling, murder and worse.

Like the novel *Rebecca,* this story, too, deals with a young girl alone in the world, cast adrift in an unfamiliar, hostile environment. Daphne du Maurier's descriptions of the moor are undoubtedly some of the finest in any Cornish novel. Here, too, she builds up an impressive portrait of Cornwall in the 1700s; at a deeper level we feel the loneliness of the moor and the sense of fear and isolation that Mary Yelland must have felt. Throughout this tale many of the characters are loathsome — with no sympathy from the reader — and her superlative story-telling enables us to share the predicament in which Mary Yelland finds herself. Sent to bed by her Uncle Joss, Mary hears strange sounds and, through a crack in her blind, she sees strange bundles being carried to and fro. One cannot help

LEFT: Maureen O'Hara played Mary Yelland in the Hitchcock film – Daphne du Maurier thought she was wonderful in the part.

BODMIN FLY

remembering the line of poetry: 'Watch the Wall my Darling as the Gentlemen go By.'

Daphne herself visited Bolventor in the 1930s. She told me, 'I got the idea for the novel *Jamaica Inn* during an expedition with my friend Foy Quiller-Couch when we visited Jamaica Inn on horseback and during the evening I began to read *Treasure Island* and that is whcn the characters began to develop and the idea of *Jamaica Inn,* with wrecking and smuggling became clear to me. My meeting with the parson from Altarnun helped me formulate the story and somehow the characters began to develop in my subconscious and I clearly imagined the vicar in a more sinister role.'

It was mid November and during the day Daphne and Foy visited some of the wellknown spots including Dozmary Pool and the church at Altarnun. At Altarnun they had made friends with the local parson and during the evening he came to visit both girls at Jamaica Inn where they

LEFT: Jamaica Inn, arguably the most famous inn in the British Isles – thanks to Daphne du Maurier's bestselling novel. The bars here are based on the story: Joss's Bar, named after the coarse brutal landlord Joss Merlyn, Mary's Bar named after Mary Yelland and the heroine from Helford, Smugglers' Bar and Stable Bar. Time was when Jamaica Inn was a posting house when the turnpike across the Moor was laid, and landlords kept horses and provided accommodation for travellers.

Why Jamaica Inn?

The name dates back to 1789. One theory is that it sold Jamaican rum. But Cornish historian H. L. Douch thinks it is so unlike Jamaica that someone thought it worth a cynical comment – and the name stuck.

talked long into the night by a large warm peat fire. All of which helped to fire Daphne's imagination as the tale began to form in her mind.

When the book was published it was a great popular success and the film rights were soon sold. Before leaving for America Alfred Hitchcock had rather rashly agreed to film *Jamaica Inn* — he had been friendly with Sir Gerald du Maurier and though claiming no special affection for her work, he went on to film three du Maurier novels. Indeed, over the years Hitchcock became famous for his treatment of du Maurier's work. Charles Laughton and Erich Pommer had snatched up the film rights to the du Maurier novel and Laughton was already cast as the star. Laughton and Hitchcock had a good deal in common: they were exactly the same age and both large men who came from comfortable middle-class backgrounds.

In some ways *Jamaica Inn* prefaces *Rebecca* published in 1938 and to be Hitchcock's next film. However Hitchcock quickly realised that

David Clarke captures Jamaica Inn today. It was here that Daphne du Maurier talked with the parson from Altarnun and the story began to form in her mind.

Jamaica Inn 'was an absurd thing to undertake'. Setting up the production was thwart with problems and the screen play was rewritten by Sidney Gillat, Daphne having declined the opportunity. At Charles Laughton's request, J.B. Priestley was brought in to specifically build up the squire's role. Hitchcock felt the novel's one redeeming feature was that it was a whodunnit. The landlord was obviously only a henchman, whereas the head of the smugglers was a man of substance — in the novel the parson. But Laughton had the story changed and in his new role as squire he replaced the parson as leader of the smugglers. With this change much of the power of the original novel was lost.

RIGHT: **Felicity Young's drawing of 'The Cathedral of the Moor' at Altarnun. The parish of Altarnun, sprawling over 15,000 acres, is the biggest in all Cornwall. It is said Sabine Baring-Gould discovered a house nearby containing a secret chamber, hidden at the back of the hearth – a nook for smuggled spirits and tobacco?**

Hereabouts fact and fiction could be curiously entwined. Long ago, ponies, laden with contraband, almost certainly travelled these narrow twisting lanes, at early hours and preferably under night's black cloak.

In the author's imagination, Francis Davey became the Vicar of Altarnun. Davey, with his white hair and a prominent thin nose 'like the curved beak of a bird', was a Devil in a dog collar. No more evil, more enigmatic character peoples the pages of any of her novels. He may be a fictitious character, but I feel his spirit still haunts the Moor, and often think of him as I come through the lovely village of Altarnun. The vicarage is now a guest house, but the parish church still dominates the villagescape. Dedicated to St Nonna, it is the Cathedral of the Moor. Its beautiful tower, spearing 130 feet into the sky, took more than a generation to build.

RIGHT: The tors of Bodmin Moor have long appealed to Dame Daphne – she used them tellingly in 'Jamaica Inn'. Stones, shaped by Nature's own sculptural genius, had an especial appeal. Brown Willy is the Cornish Everest. Here is a view of this majestic tor caught, from a distance, by the camera of Ray Bishop, a man who has been photographing the Moor in its varying moods for more than forty years.

The old Rectory of Altarnun, a rarely photographed aspect of the du Maurier locations in Cornwall. Photographer Ray Bishop visited it on a brilliant September morning in 1987, only days before the property changed ownership. Daphne du Maurier would have seen it, and almost certainly called here, on her visit to Altarnun all those years ago. The village and the vicar clearly made a great impact, for she used both significantly in 'Jamaica Inn'.

Of the film Daphne du Maurier said: 'I was not consulted. I thought the wrecking scene at the beginning good, but I think they could have done a lot more with the story. In fact, they changed the theme and this affected the plot.' Because of the changes in both the characters and plot, it would seem Hitchcock tackled the film lackadaisically: there were also rumours that Hitchcock and Laughton fell out during the production. For all its faults *Jamaica Inn,* made in 1939, had a star-studded cast including Charles Laughton, Leslie Banks, Emlyn Williams, Robert Newton and Maureen O'Hara. This film gave Maureen O'Hara her first major film role, but Hitchcock's relationship with her was distant and as usual he was more interested in the mechanics of film-making than looking after the performances of individual actors. On release *Jamaica Inn* was a considerable box office success, enhancing du Maurier's reputation and paving the way for her considerable popularity as an author in the United States.

Dozmary Pool, shown on the previous page, appears in the novel 'Jamaica Inn'. It is one of the loveliest, most surprising features of Bodmin Moor. In her book 'Vanishing Cornwall' Daphne du Maurier referred to its 'many moods' and gave it the old spelling of Dozmare.

It is a magical place. In its placid mood, Dozmary becomes a mirror reflecting the moor around it and the sky above. On other days it has a different power and yet C. E. Vulliamy, a fine descriptive writer, who came to the Pool more than fifty years ago, confessed: '... so elusive, that it can only be conveyed to you in pictures: thc limits of descriptive writing are soon exhausted.'

There is an Arthurian echo here, and Sally Jones, in her 'Legends of Cornwall', evoked that echo:

'To me Dozmary has always been the most beautiful and eerie part of the moor, fed by no obvious streams or springs but appearing naturally in the windswept natural basin.

'The legends are an organic part of the scene. The least imaginative would invent them if the lake were not already haunted by the ghosts of Tregeagle, and Sir Bedivere who after some controversy, returned Arthur's great sword Excalibur to the Lady of the Lake. Bedivere carried the dying

Arthur away after the Battle of Camlann, and the King ordered him to throw Excalibur into the nearby pool. Bedivere took the sword and hid it, then returned to his master who asked him what he had seen. 'Nothing except the ripples on the lake,' said Bedivere. The King was furious and raged at the knight for deceiving him, commanding him to take the sword again and carry out his orders to the letter. Bedivere again went away and again hid Excalibur, thinking it a terrible waste to throw the bejewelled weapon away.

When he returned to Arthur with the same story as before, the King was more furious than ever and threatened to hurl Excalibur into Dozmary himself and then kill Bedivere with his bare hands, in spite of his dreadful wounds.

At this Bedivere realised that his mission had a deeper, more mystical significance than he had imagined, so he did as he was told, and in the simple prose of Malory, 'threw the sword into the water as far as he might, and there came an arm and a hand above the water and met it and caught it, and so shook it thrice and brandished. And then the hand vanished away with the sword in the water.

'So the sword which the Lady of the Lake had given Arthur, vanished into the deep again as mysteriously as it had come.'

Rebecca

Rebecca is one of the great bestsellers in the history of publishing, read and enjoyed in many languages. It has been outstanding at five levels: as a novel, as a film, as a play, as a television series and even as an opera. First published in 1938 it was an immediate popular success both in Britain and in North America.

In Britain alone during its first year of publication millions of people took it to heart, identifying strongly with the predicament of the nameless heroine, for ever shadowed by the menacing ghostly presence of the dead Rebecca.

The story of *Rebecca* could be likened to classical tales such as *Cinderella* and *Jane Eyre* — a fact confirmed in an early line of Jack Favell to Mrs Danvers: 'Careful Danny, we don't want to shock Cinderella, do we?' From her first appearance, the housekeeper Mrs Danvers could almost be thought of as one of the ugly sisters and Jack Favell is an ally of hers.

Rebecca concerns itself with the story of a gauche young girl who meets sophisticated and mysterious Mr Maxim de Winter holidaying on the French Riviera. Maxim is seemingly there to recover from the death of his beautiful wife, Rebecca, while the nameless heroine is the companion of the odious and vulgar Mrs van Hopper. A whirlwind romance develops; Maxim marries the girl and they return to his family home, Manderley, in Cornwall. Here, the nervous young girl, suddenly elevated to the status of mistress of the household, finds herself confronted by the sinister Mrs Danvers, the housekeeper who adored Rebecca. As time goes on, she becomes terrified by Mrs Danvers who keeps the rooms where Rebecca lived exactly as they were when she was alive — especially Rebecca's bedroom in the west wing.

Joan Fontaine and Judith Anderson in the balcony scene in the 1940 film of 'Rebecca'.

Milton, near Peterborough. Some of the rooms were used by Daphne for the interior scenes of Manderley.

When walking round the grounds of Manderley, the young girl discovers the beach house where Rebecca once entertained her friends. It would be here later that Maxim would tell her how he killed Rebecca and why he did not love her.

Preparing for a ball at Manderley, Mrs Danvers advises her to wear a dress copied from one of the family portraits. Unwittingly she therefore wears the same dress that Rebecca had worn. When Maxim sees his second wife thus dressed he becomes furious. During the party a boat is wrecked in the bay. Divers go down and another boat is found – Rebecca's – her body still inside and an inquest is demanded. Maxim now has to explain how and why he identified another woman's body as his wife Rebecca. Through Mrs Danvers, Maxim and his second wife find the name of Rebecca's doctor in London. They eventually track down the doctor who explains that Rebecca actually did not have long to live. She had cancer and suicide was then judged to be the case.

Jack Favell rings Mrs Danvers at Manderley and tells her the news. The housekeeper goes insane and sets fire to the house. As Maxim drives westward back to Manderley he sees the crimson sky.

In terms of sheer construction Rebecca is another interesting mixture of fact and fiction. The house of Manderley, which is a central plank of the whole story, is a combination of two real houses: Milton near Peterborough and Menabilly hard by Fowey. Daphne told me: 'The entrance hall at Milton was exactly as I described in *Rebecca,* when the second wife arrives for the first time at Manderley, and meets the household staff: the only difference being that I described a sweeping staircase coming down into a hallway.' Therefore some of the rooms at Milton and several portraits were used by Daphne to describe the interior of her fictional house Manderley. The author had, in fact, visited Milton twice in her childhood and the place must have made a tremendous impression – for the memory of those two visits stayed with her all her life. The whole atmosphere of Milton during Daphne's visit would have been very formal and correct: a full house staff of butler, housmaid, cook and housekeeper. It is therefore interesting to reflect that in *Rebecca* the housekeeper plays such an important, significant part.

During 1917 the housekeeper was a Miss Parker, who was described as 'tall, dark and very commanding'. She could indeed be Mrs Danvers

ABOVE: **'Rebecca' has become a spectacular part of publishing history. One of the world's bestsellers, it has been read and hugely enjoyed in many languages. This apparently secret house, tucked away in romantic Cornish woodlands within the sound of the sea – this real place almost too idyllic to be true – was largely the Manderley of the story: another example of Dame Daphne's brilliance in turning living reality into memorable fiction. Menabilly, in addition to being a fine old Cornish house belonging to a famous Cornish family, is an insight into the author. Menabilly is a monument to Dame Daphne's craft. Here Daphne walks with her daughter Flavia and grandchildren in front of the house.**

LEFT: **The entrance to Menabilly which inspired that magnificent opening sentence of the novel 'Rebecca'.**

Polridmouth Bay, its beautiful beach house and lake combine to make a setting that is almost too pretty to be true. This location Dame Daphne used for several key scenes in 'Rebecca'.

and Daphne had this to say about the housekeeper: 'I had seen the black dress and the chain with keys on a housekeeper in one of the houses I stayed at. It could have been Milton or another house. The rest of the description is imaginary.'

The setting for the novel *Rebecca* is largely the grounds around her former home Menabilly, near Fowey. The beach house beneath Menabilly is the beach house described in *Rebecca*. Polridmouth Bay is also the scene for Rebecca's murder and the wreck of her boat.

Daphne and her sister Angela first discovered Menabilly in the early 1930s during a summer expedition walking around the coastline near Fowey, but they found that to get to the house they needed to walk down an overgrown drive about three miles long — the entrance being at the crossroads at Four Turnings. It was to be this journey through the

overgrown drive, twisting and turning, and apparently impassable that Daphne was to describe in the poignant beginning to her novel when she wrote the now famous words, 'Last night I dreamt I went to Manderley again.'

On another visit to Fowey the following year, Daphne finally discovered Menabilly and she found, at long last, her mysterious house of secrets which was to inspire her to write not only *Rebecca* but which she also used in her other Cornish novels *My Cousin Rachel, The King's General* and *Frenchman's Creek.*

Daphne once told me, when driving me back to my hotel in Fowey, all about the drive at the beginning of *Rebecca.* As we came to Four Turnings she said: 'That is the drive I had in mind when I wrote *Rebecca,* you know "Last night I dreamt . . . "'

Polridmouth Bay, with Gribbin Head in the background, scene of murder and wreck in the novel.

After this discovery of Menabilly, which in those days was neglected and covered in ivy, Daphne would often, in her own words, trespass in the grounds for hours at a time. Then she wrote to the owners asking for permission to trespass in the woods around Menabilly and they generously gave their consent. Eventually the owners allowed her to take on a long-term lease of the property and residence at Menabilly began in 1943. It was to last for twenty-four years ending in a move to Kilmarth in 1967.

When she first lived at Menabilly everyone thought she was mad because the house was neglected and run-down, but after a few months, the ivy was removed, the roof repaired and life appeared in the building once again. Daphne lived here with her husband 'Boy Browning' and their children, two girls and a boy. Although she was now married with a growing family to care for, Daphne's imagination was not dampened or her enthusiasm for writing diminished. She had placed a small summer house in the grounds in which to work.

It was, of course, more than the house that fascinated her, there was the history of the Rashleigh family who, for generations, had occupied Menabilly — and who were destined to appear again and again in her novels in one disguise or another.

Then there were the Quiller-Couches who told Daphne about one member of the Rashleigh family who had been married first to a very beautiful wife, whom he had divorced, and then he married a very much younger woman. Ideas began to develop in Daphne's imagination. There had been a wreck in the bay at Polridmouth — also down on the shore was a beach or boathouse. So the basic story began to germinate. Some years later and after her marriage to soldier, 'Boy Browning', Daphne was

Menabilly was neglected and covered in ivy when Daphne took on a long-term lease in 1943.

stationed with her husband in Alexandria, Egypt, and she began to feel homesick for Cornwall. Her obsession with Menabilly began to surface in both her thinking and her writing, and it was here in Egypt that she started the novel *Rebecca,* remembering her beloved Cornwall — and maybe distance and longing sharpening her memory and imagery. Returning to England, the Brownings were stationed at Aldershot, where they rented a house called Greyfriars, near Fleet. Here she completed the novel. Daphne told me: 'I began the novel in the first person and I avoided giving the heroine a name because it became an interesting exercise in writing and technique.'

Upon publication, the novel became an instant success here and in North America. Serialised in the newspapers, it whetted readers' appetites, and the radio première of the story, produced by Orson Welles, who also starred in the production in December 1938, made a listening public keen to see the film version. The film rights were sold to David Selznick by Daphne's agent, Curtis Brown, and it was announced that Alfred Hitchcock would direct. Laurence, now Lord Olivier, would star alongside a newcomer Joan Fontaine, who was Olivia de Havilland's sister. The rest of the cast included Daphne's old friend Gladys Cooper as Bea, Judith Anderson as Mrs Danvers and George Sanders as Jack Favell. Hitchcock, this time, followed the story faithfully, careful to retain the fairytale elements. He also did not want to lose the rococo Englishness which made *Rebecca* so attractive. The film therefore is Hitchcock at his most masterly: though he had some reservations about the film, it stands as a supreme example of his craft. Moreover the success of this film all over the world confirmed Daphne du Maurier's place among the popular authors of the twentieth century. The film won an Oscar for the Best Film and there was an Oscar nomination for Joan Fontaine.

Joan Fontaine told me: 'During the filming of *Rebecca* there was tension and I did feel just like that little nobody in the story, but this helped me with the part. You see, Larry Olivier actually wanted his wife Vivien Leigh to play the part of his second wife.' Laurence Olivier, for his part, has said: 'Without my success in *Rebecca* I would certainly never have become an international filmstar.' During the production of the film in Hollywood, Daphne was asked to go and oversee filming, but she declined and wrote to David Selznick saying: 'I would prefer that the

OVERLEAF: **Joan Fontaine in the film is frightened by the housekeeper in Rebecca's bedroom – the only room that looks down to the sea.**

BELOW: **Laurence Olivier in 'Rebecca' 1940.**

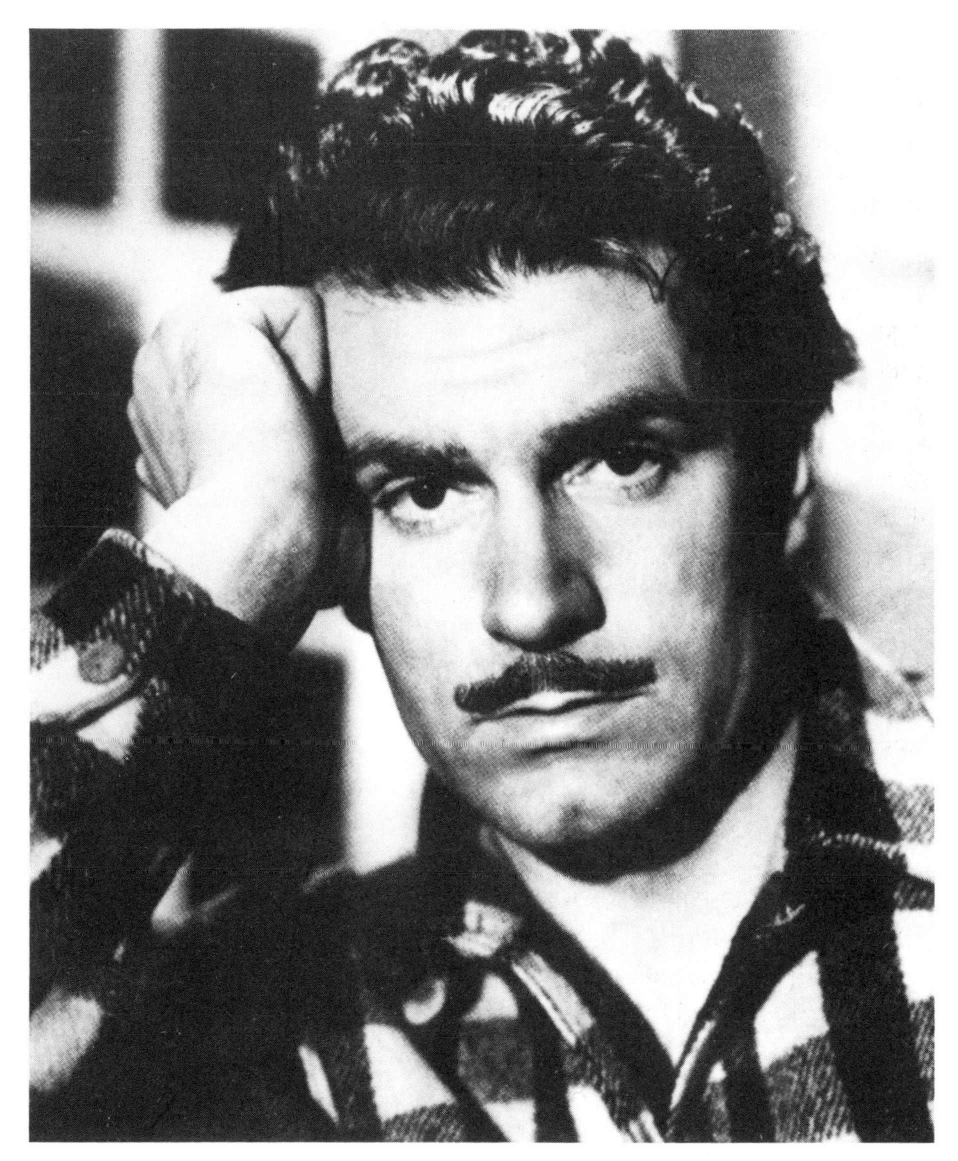

A sketch made for the Hitchcock film of Manderley after the fire.

character of Rebecca is not shown in the film as this would completely undo the plot.'

The production of *Rebecca* greatly pleased Daphne and she rates it the most successful adaptation of any of her books, and she could not fault the casting of the film at all.

During recent years the television companies have produced several adaptations of some of du Maurier's most famous novels. This all began with the BBC television production of *Rebecca*. This was the first time that one of her stories was filmed in actual Cornish locations, and the whole production benefitted from this. Caerhays Castle was used as the fictional house, Manderley, and the surrounding coastline played an active part in this story of suspense and drama. Daphne said about the series: 'When people watch this production of *Rebecca* they imagine I am sitting at home with a butler at my side, holding a silver tray, and here I am boiling an egg for my supper! On the whole, I thought the production quite good. Joanna David was really rather smashing, but again, I did think that the Hitchcock film was awfully well done and that takes some beating.' Many close friends of du Maurier thought that Joanna David bore a remarkable resemblance to the young Daphne.

When asked today about the success of this particular novel, Daphne replied: 'I could never understand why it became so popular. I still get letters about the novel and this is why I published the Rebecca Notebook.' Fifty years on it remains a beautifully crafted and highly evocative novel. The lush growth of rhododendrons and hydrangeas vividly described in her text; tea on the lawn with the sound of the sea coming up from the shore; birds singing at dawn and rooks circling around the trees; the cottage in the cove: these are only some of the images which show her masterly talent of capturing mood and subtlety.

Caerhays Castle is Manderley – well, almost Manderley, for it was the inspired choice of set for the refilming of Daphne du Maurier's 'Rebecca' for BBC television.

Caerhays is one of Cornwall's most beautiful, delightful surprises. Sir John Betjeman, touring Cornwall in the early 1960s, spoke of 'the sudden opening on to the grey towers and turrets of Caerhays, John Nash's fanciful and only surviving Gothick Castle . . .'

Nash, the architect of Buckingham Palace, built it in 1808 and even today – perhaps more so today – it has a fairytale quality.

It is the home of Julian Williams, Chairman of Cornwall County Council and a member of Prince Charles's Council which administers the Duchy of Cornwall. The Castle is never open to the public, but the gardens, considered among the finest in the land, are usually open for charity – at Easter and Whitsun.

Caerhays is the site of the old home of the Trevanions. They have been a great Cornish family through generations – and one of them brought home Nelson's despatches from Trafalgar. Another, Hugh Trevanion, was knighted on Bosworth Field by Henry VII. All that belongs to history and Daphne du Maurier, with her imagination and feeling for the past, has included the Trevanion family in 'The King's General', her novel of the Civil War.

Just below Caerhays is Porthluney Beach, still one of the most romantic beaches in all Cornwall. It was the film location for the opening sequence of 'Poldark', the highly successful TV series of some ten years ago, based on the novels of Winston Graham.

The genesis of Daphne du Maurier's short story, 'The Birds', was here in Cornwall: a farming scene very like Ray Bishop's photograph of ploughing on a Cornish farm in autumn. From this seemingly ordinary country activity, Daphne du Maurier's imagination and her gift for dragging up those irrational fears that lurk inside many of us combined to create something special.

The original story 'The Birds' deals with one farmer, Nat Hocken and his family and is set in du Maurier's beloved rural Cornwall. The farm at Menabilly Barton is the actual setting. The Hockens are besieged in their farmhouse, as millions of birds inexplicably start attacking humans. The sheer weight of the birds destroys RAF planes, and the story ends with Nat smoking his last cigarette, the radio silent, and the birds outside massing for their final attack. This strange haunting fantasy of birds combining to wipe out humanity appealed to Alfred Hitchcock – and the result is a classic horror film, his third du Maurier story.

Cinematically the story presented a tantalizing problem: how to convey a world threatened by the most benign of creatures – the bird. Hitchcock changed the location to California and a lot of the action took place around San Francisco.

"It could be
the most
terrifying
motion
picture
I have
ever made!"

Alfred J. Hitchcock

Tippi Hedren in a dramatic scene from 'The Birds'.

Frenchman's Creek

Frenchman's Creek was first published in 1941 and immediately romance and adventure turned it into a highly popular novel. For nearly half a century it has been a well-loved title, read and enjoyed all over the world. Rightly, if somewhat pompously, did the *Sunday Times* predict: 'A heroine who is bound to make thousands of friends in spite of her somewhat questionable behaviour. It is set in and around the Helford River and you can find Frenchman's Creek on the map of Cornwall near Helford Village.

Daphne du Maurier may have set *her story* back in history but its magic still works today. Sarah Foot visiting in 1984 for her book *Rivers of Cornwall* reflected: 'As soon as we reached Frenchman's Creek I felt we

Dame Daphne and her husband, after their wedding at Lanteglos Church, in their boat headed for the open sea, destined for Helford and Frenchman's Creek. 'We couldn't have chosen anything more beautiful,' Dame Daphne reflected 45 years later.

Frenchman's Creek – there's a magical ring in the name – but locally it's been known as Frenchman's Pill or quite simply Pill: the Cornish word for creek.

were entering a part of the river that was out of bounds. We were intruders.'

Local people, though, are cautious about entering Frenchman's Creek, many of them believing it is 'spooked'. The truth is it has a genuinely haunted reputation in that an old man, taking a short cut across the creek, did not return home one night. In the morning they found him sitting upright in the river, dead, with his hat still on his head, and his long white beard running with water. In a strange way he lives on

'As soon as we reached Frenchman's Creek, I felt we were entering a part of the river that was out of bounds. We were the intruders.'

That was Sarah Foot's reaction when she sailed there for the first time and described it in 'Rivers of Cornwall'.

The beautiful Lady St Columb is probably one of Daphne du Maurier's most endearing female characters. In flight from the Court of Charles II, jaded by its character and weary of a stupid husband, she longs for a new life in Cornwall in the house on the Helford – the property of her husband's family, but which she has never seen. From the moment she arrives here, she feels a strange sense of peace and a gripping story unfolds.

in that his ghost has appeared in local cottages and houses he knew in his lifetime.

As for the novel this is Daphne du Maurier at her Cornish best. She opens with the east wind blowing up Helford River when the waters become troubled and stirred as does the life of the heroine, beautiful Lady Dona. For while the gentry strive to capture a Frenchman who plunders their coastline, Lady Dona finds excitement and passion as she dares to love a pirate.

In it, though, are many references to Philip Rashleigh who lived at Fowey and in one section Dona joins the French pirate in a raid on Fowey harbour where they capture Philip Rashleigh's boat and set out to sea in it. Daphne du Maurier had this to say recently in a conversation: 'The story

Fowey Harbour, where Dona St Columb joins in a pirate raid and captures Philip Rashleigh's boat.

on the whole was largely imaginary. The house Navron was based on one of the old houses on the Helford River and this is the closest I have come to writing a romantic novel . . .'

The success of the novel resulted in the film rights soon being sold to America. Joan Fontaine was cast in the exciting role of Dona St Columb while Basil Rathbone and Reginald Denny were in the cast alongside Arturo de Cordova who played the pirate. Daphne has told me, 'My husband loved the film because the music used on the sound track was *Clair de Lune*, and Joan Fontaine told me, 'We couldn't film in Cornwall at the time because of the war, so we went to the north of California where you have inlets covered with trees growing down to the water's edge and actually it looks a lot like Cornwall.'

Joan Fontaine played Dona St Columb in the film of 'Frenchman's Creek'. Here she is in a scene with Basil Rathbone.

LEFT: The Author, Martyn Shallcross, interviewing Joan Fontaine at the National Film Theatre in 1978. Daphne du Maurier introduced them.

The King's General

The novels of Daphne du Maurier grew from a very definite pattern. She once explained: 'I have to think about it for months . . . nothing on paper, just thoughts. Then I do a draft of notes; a skeleton if you like. I go through each chapter, and then re-read the book as a whole.'

The King's General she finished rapidly: a matter of just three months. She wrote it during the last war and reflected: 'I think the anxiety one feels in wartime helped me to write this book. My husband was abroad at the time and I think I caught the spirit of war in that book.' The novel is dedicated to her husband in rather amusing form: 'To my husband, also a general, but, I trust, a more discreet one.' Sir Frederick Browning did, of course, enjoy a distinguished Army career. A Commander of the British Airborne Corps, he won the DSO and later served as Treasurer to the Duke of Edinburgh. On retiring and settling in Cornwall, he became a member of Cornwall County Council.

After *The King's General* the time spent on each novel increased significantly. The later titles took her six to seven months. When actually engaged on a book, a regular work pattern emerged. Usually she wrote from 10.30 a.m. to 1p.m. and from 5.30 to 7.30 p.m. Sometimes she worked for a while in the afternoon but, weather permitting, she normally went for walks.

The story of *The King's General* uses many splendid Cornish locations in story and plot and it is a tragedy that the novel never became a film. After Daphne du Maurier had completed it, Sir Alexander Korda sent a film crew down to Cornwall to film the author at work at Menabilly. Sadly the film was due to go into production when something happened and the project fell through. In a conversation with Stewart Granger, he told me:

Tywardreath at 12 noon in 1987. This is a Cornish parish steeped in history. Menabilly, home of the Rashleighs, sixteenth-century, eighteenth-century and Regency, stands inside its boundaries. Gribbin Head, with its slate cliffs, is another impressive landmark. This parish, more than any other in all Cornwall, has fired the imagination of Daphne du Maurier. It lost a priory under Henry VIII and most of its church in the last century. In the churchyard lie the bones of a man who died in 1655. Robert Harris, a major-general of His Majesty's forces, had to flee for his life in the Civil War, leaving behind all his valuables. Many, many years later labourers, working on an old hedge in the parish, discovered a number of silver bowls and dishes. They bore the armorial bearings of the Harrises. It is that kind of place.

'The King's General' is a magnificent blend of fact and fiction in which Daphne du Maurier tells the story of her Cornish home Menabilly during the Civil War. A reviewer in Queen magazine wrote of her skill: 'With a sensitive hand and deft imagination she spins . . . a fascinating cobweb of romance and drama . . .'

Pendennis Castle at the mouth of the River Fal is another Cornish fortress featured in 'The King's General'. Historically, Pendennis is remembered as one of the longest sieges of the Civil War. Surrender, though, was inevitable but the 24 officers and 900 other survivors marched out on the day of the surrender with 'colours flying, trumpet sounding, drums beating, matches lighted at both ends, bullets in their mouths, and every soldier twelve charges of powder'. It must have been a highly emotional occasion as many of the men were so weak from starvation they died soon afterwards. Little wonder then there are stories of dead soldiers haunting the castle and grounds.

'The only story I was due to do of Daphne's was *The King's General,* and I was to have played the part of Sir Richard Grenvile.'

This, Daphne du Maurier's fifth novel, is set during the Civil War: a brilliant recreation of the love shared by Sir Richard Grenvile — the King's General in the West — and Honor Harris, as courageous as she was beautiful, during the war when Cornwall echoed to Royalist drums and rebel bugles. But this is more than a moving love story, for the novel underlines Dame Daphne's sense of history. She resurrects seventeenth-century Cornwall with insight. One episode relates to her own neck of the Cornish woods — that narrow neck of land between Fowey and Par — where the Parliamentary forces under the Earl of Essex fought a hopeless battle at Castle Dor, and the pages are peppered with historic locations spilling over into Devon: places like Plymouth and Tavistock. But the heart and soul of the story is here in Cornwall: red crosses on the maps, marking the beaches where the invading troops should land: Veryan, Pentewan and Crinnis. Beacons on the headlands: The Nare, The Dodman and The Gribben. Great Cornish families people the pages: the Arundells of Trerice, the Trelawnys of Trelawne, Sir Arthur Basset of Tehidy and Sir Charles Trevanion of Caerhays, although you will find different spellings of people and places in the novel.

An intriguing postscript to the novel is that in 1824 Mr William Rashleigh of Menabilly had certain alterations made to the house and, in the process, masons uncovered a small room or cell. In it they found the skeleton of a young man seated on a stool dressed in the clothes of a Cavalier, as worn during the days of the Civil War. On consulting family records, William Rashleigh discovered that members of the Grenvile family had hidden at Menabilly before the rising of 1648. He surmised one had taken refuge in that secret room — and had been forgotten.

My Cousin Rachel

Speaking to *The Cornish Magazine* in 1963, Dame Daphne said: 'Each book has given me pleasure but, you know, when it's completed the whole thing fades. Each has its phase. What you want to write about changes with the years. *My Cousin Rachel* possibly marked the end of a phase . . . I cannot see myself settling down to another Cornish novel.'

Though *The House on the Strand* and *Rule Britannia* were yet to come, *My Cousin Rachel* was, in fact, the end of an era: her last truly historical novel set in Cornwall. *The House on the Strand* hovered between past and present, and *Rule Britannia* was set in the future. So *My Cousin Rachel* is an important volume in the du Maurier story.

First published in 1951, it has a Jane Eyre quality of suspense and ultimate tragedy. A reviewer for the magazine *Queen* referred to it as 'dramatic, surprising and masterly . . . a highly skilled piece of story-telling.' Many of her readers might well vote this their favourite Cornish novel for it is vintage du Maurier: mystery and murder mingling. The story opens with another memorable sentence: 'They used to hang men at Four Turnings in the old days.'

Ambrose married Rachel, Countess Sangalletti, in Italy and never returned home. His letters to his cousin Philip hinted that he was being poisoned, and when Philip gets to Italy it is too late. Ambrose is already dead. Then Rachel crosses the English Channel; comes to Cornwall and Philip finds himself torn between dark suspicion and passionate love. Is she a scheming murderess? Or is she the angelic woman she often seems?

LEFT: **Richard Burton and Olivia de Havilland star in 'My Cousin Rachel'.**

The Rashleigh family name was used again as the fictional character's surname in the novel. In the story the name was changed to Ashley. Philip Ashley lived in a beautiful manor house in Cornwall, which had extensive grounds, full of rhododendron bushes. Daphne told me: 'So much of Rachel was imagined at my then home Menabilly; the idea for the sunken garden which would cause Rachel's death came to me one afternoon whilst out walking near Menabilly.'

Soon after the novel was published, the film rights were sold to America, and the possibilities for a great dramatic part for a slightly older actress were apparent.

During the following month the celebrated film director George Cukor, well-known as a woman's director, came down to Cornwall and visited Daphne to discuss filming *Rachel.* He planned to use the enigmatic Swedish star, the celebrated Greta Garbo, in the part of Rachel. This was to have been Garbo's return to the screen after an absence of several years. Unfortunately this was not to be and the film went on to be made with Richard Burton as Philip Ashley and Joan Fontaine's sister Olivia de Havilland as Rachel.

Daphne had this to say about the film: 'I never thought Olivia de Havilland quite the person I imagined as Rachel. I actually would have liked Vivien Leigh to have played the part; she told me in New York that she would love to play the part, she would have been splendid as Rachel.'

Pan, her paperback publishers, wisely used Geraldine Chaplin as Rachel on the cover, Miss Chaplin having starred in that role in the BBC TV production, produced by Richard Beyon and directed by Brian Farnham. It made splendid television, and Geraldine Chaplin makes an inspired cover for the paperback version.

RIGHT: **A family group, taken at Menabilly in September 1944. Daphne du Maurier holding her son Christian – nicknamed 'Kits' – aged 3; Tessa, the elder girl aged 11 years and Flavia 7 years old. Menabilly once again was the setting for her last Cornish historical novel.**

Throughout the novel the prose is typically Daphne du Maurier: clear-cut and assured. The characters speak, act and react in such a way that we hurry from page to page. If this were the end of a Cornish innings, then Daphne du Maurier completed it with style — and story-telling brilliance.

She opened the story sharply and ended with the same telling effect: 'They used to hang men at Four Turnings in the old days.

'Not any more, though.'

LEFT: The genesis of the novel 'My Cousin Rachel' was the result of Daphne du Maurier visiting Antony House in south-east Cornwall about 1950. She liked to take a character from a well-known Cornish family and house and here her choice was Rachel Carew around whom she created the fictional story. The portrait of Rachel Carew, which inspired her, still hangs in the Porch Room at Antony. It was painted by Mary Beale, who was something of a pioneer in that she was one of the first women professional painters. It should, though, be stressed that Rachel Carew was not in the least like her counterpart in the novel. She married Ambrose Manaton of Kilworthy and died young.

BELOW: Four Turnings in 1987 – a far cry from the place where they once hanged offenders. This is an early morning picture in autumn, when Cornish roads are often quiet and sometimes deserted.

The Tristan Stone is an example of how legend is very alive in Cornwall. On the road to Fowey, on the left hand side before you start dropping down into the town, you'll find this seven-feet-tall monolith.

An inscription running in two lines down one face of the stone, reads: 'DRUSTANUS HIC IACIT CUNOMORI FILIUS' meaning 'Here lies Tristan, son of Cunomorus'. Drustanus is the sixth-century name for Tristan and Cunomorus, or Cynvawr, interestingly was one of the sixth-century kings of Dumnonia – and Cornwall was part of the kingdom of Dumnonia. Today's traveller is therefore truly on Royal ground.

Castle Dor

Castle Dor is a rare collaboration between a living author and a dead writer.

This is a retelling – nineteenth-century Cornwall and its people and one of the saddest love stories the world has ever known.

Foy Quiller-Couch, daughter of the celebrated Sir Arthur Quiller-Couch, told my publisher Michael Williams how this book came about. She recalled how back in the 1920s she had ridden with her father up to Lantyan. The great man was already in the grip of the fascination of blending the legend of Tristan and Iseult and the Fowey River. But it was a book and a theme for vacations. The great man was then at Cambridge and it was only in those precious holidays, back in Cornwall, that he was able to devote time and energy to this favourite theme. Yet curiously, Foy Quiller-Couch expressed the belief that her father somehow tired of the subject or, at least, felt that the manuscript would never be good enough to publish. This upset her greatly and, interestingly, when Sir Arthur died in 1944 this unfinished manuscript came into her possession. In a way it was a fortunate act because daughter reversed father's decision. It was not, however, until 1959 when rereading the manuscript that she asked her friend Daphne du Maurier to complete it. She told Michael Williams: 'Daphne did it so brilliantly, weaving her words into his, that I believe no reader will know where and when the shuttle was transferred from my father's hand into hers.'

When Michael Williams interviewed Daphne du Maurier she confessed that her immediate reaction had been to say no, but that on reading the manuscript she too felt the spell and the magic of the story and therefore responded to the challenge. Moreover, she was under the very definite view that Doctor Carfax, a central character, was largely Q himself.

Sir Arthur Quiller-Couch, one of the great characters of Cornish literature. Q was the author of many novels based on his beloved Fowey and the original editor of 'The Oxford Book of English Verse'. Dining with Q and his family remained a vivid memory for Daphne du Maurier (right). Recalling her early contacts with them, she once said: 'It could be a bit frightening; in a way you sat on the edge of your chair. The old man could be very Victorian. He was inclined to switch, broad-minded one moment and very rigid the next.' Our photograph shows Sir Arthur on the eve of his 80th birthday on 21 November 1943, in the study of his house, The Haven, overlooking Fowey Harbour. A Q paperweight lies on his desk.

The remains of Castle Dore stand in a green field by the road linking Fowey and Lostwithiel. There is frankly nothing dramatic about the site today – all that remains is a large rough circle of banks and ditches. The romance of the place is that when Castle Dore was excavated half a century ago, it was discovered the fort had been reoccupied during the Dark Ages, the time of King Arthur. Was this then the legendary palace of King Mark?

Mary and Hal Price in their 'Castles of Cornwall', published by Bossiney, have written:

'All round the site were dwellings, stables and storerooms of Celtic chieftains who ruled there. Other than the post holes the archaeologists found no more than a few handfuls of beads of that period. Time had eroded all other evidence of those who had once lived there in the time of Arthur.

'There is a sense of peace and romance about Castle Dore which makes it easy to accept the legend of the tragic lovers. Tristram and Iseult, who, it is believed, once lived there. Castle Dore, the old story tells us, was the home of King Mark of Cornwall, the uncle of Tristram and the husband of Iseult.

'It was to Castle Dore that Tristram escorted from Ireland the young and beautiful Iseult to be his uncle's bride. But on the journey Tristram and Iseult drank the love potion intended for her and King Mark on their wedding

night. In so doing they were bound in everlasting love. They kept their love a secret from the King until an enemy of Tristram within the court betrayed him. Tristram fled and took refuge from Mark's anger by hiding in the dense forest which grew near the castle. Iseult, alone and heartbroken, wandered pining for her banished knight about the castle walls. In the chapel the lovers, in death, were finally united. From Tristram's tomb there sprung a vine which spread along the walls and descended into the grave of his beloved. It was cut down three times, but each time sprung up more vigorous than before. Sadly, nothing now but the legend remains to unite these tragic lovers.'

This is Q's last novel or more accurately it is half Q's last novel as Dame Daphne took over the manuscript as it stood, which was somewhere about the halfway stage. Fortunately, Q had left a few substantial clues as to his ultimate intention. Though detection of the changeover may not be easy, readers who know their Daphne du Maurier will find greater pace and more sharply defined detail in the second half.

There is an interesting piece of literary replay in this collaboration between du Maurier and Q in that one of his earliest and most successful literary exploits was completing Robert Louis Stevenson's *St Ives.*

The genesis of *Castle Dor* is that soon after the 1914-18 war he discovered Mark's Gate on a local map and this discovery launched his search for place associations and in that search the idea of *Castle Dor* was born. Amyot, the Breton onion seller, and the beautiful and newly wed Linnet Lawherne in his imagination he brought together in a chance encounter and as the story unfolds the ancient legend takes command of reality — the principal characters finding their actions fatefully linked with the past.

Kilmarth
THE HOUSE ON THE STRAND

With her move from Menabilly in 1967 Daphne du Maurier now gave up real roots. The Rashleigh family wanted to move back to their ancestral home, and Daphne through the years had only been able to rent the estate, once reflecting: 'I could never buy the houses that I wanted . . . '

Despite the death of her husband and the scattering of her family — and maybe because of these facts — she found, to a certain disbelief, that she was starting a new beginning. This new beginning took place a little further due west from Menabilly — at Kilmarth, the former dower house to Menabilly. It is a fine old house overlooking the great sweep of Par Bay, built upon fourteenth-century foundations. The name Kilmarth in Cornish means 'Retreat of Mark'.

Once more a house began to interest Daphne, her imagination stirring images of the past, ideas gradually growing and developing into a new book.

The House on the Strand, which first saw the light of publication day in 1969, is a brilliant combination: part straight novel and part story of suspense. It has a wonderfully photographic quality, and as we travel from page to page, thanks to Daphne du Maurier's imagination and historical researches, we see Cornwall in the twentieth and fourteenth centuries.

It is a fascinating plot: Dick Young, the central character, has been lent this house on the south coast of Cornwall, by a friend who is a professor of bio-physics. Agreeing to act as a guinea pig while he is there for a new drug which Professor Lane has discovered, the bottles are waiting there for him in the laboratory at Kilmarth. Little does he know that the prescribed dose is no less than a time machine, taking him back six hundred years to the same yet different Cornish landscape. On successive days Dick Young takes successive 'trips' — always back to the same settings. Like an invisible man, he witnesses intrigue and adultery, even murder, and somehow curiously feels himself personally involved. Hallucinations? Subconscious escape from his own life today? Or has Dick really travelled back in time? This is Dame Daphne at her most beguiling. It is a kind of express train in that it gets us to a final startling climax as we hurry from page to page.

Why this book has never reached the cinema screen must remain a literary and commercial mystery.

Robin Ellis, star of the *Poldark* series, based on the bestselling novels of Winston Graham, took out an option on the story and planned to make a film of the theme in Cornwall. Daphne told me: 'Their ideas seemed to be so original, but I'm afraid the money just couldn't be raised to finance the film which was a pity.'

Around this time Daphne was lucky enough to have one of her short stories turned into another memorable film, *Don't Look Now,* which was

LEFT: **Kilmarth, where Daphne moved in 1967 and has lived ever since.**

There are references to Tywardreath in 'The House on the Strand': the monks and the Priory and the Lord of the Manor of Tywardreath. In total contrast she refers to the Tywardreath of the twentieth century: the solid parish church and the visitors who come over from Fowey and Par.

directed by the highly talented Nicholas Roeg. The film was a great success in this country and throughout Europe. Set in Venice, the content slightly horrific, the film starred Julie Christie and Donald Sutherland. It was Donald Sutherland who told me: 'I loved the film. The story had a kind of Hitchcock feel of suspense, but I'm afraid it wasn't a great success in the States which was a pity.'

Nevertheless this film reawakened interest in Daphne's short stories. It is interesting that many of her short stories have an horrific and psychic element to them — totally different from her successful Cornish novels — and often inspired by visits abroad. *Not After Midnight,* for example, was triggered by her holiday in the Greek island of Crete. She fell in love with Crete and often wished to return. On the subject of the

continued success of her short stories, Daphne told me, 'It is funny really, but the psychic element to my writing only shows itself in my short stories.'

In any assessment of Dame Daphne we should never forget her considerable talents as a short story writer.

Many of her short stories have a haunting quality. The fact that *The Birds* and *Don't Look Now* were made into outstanding films for the cinema screen underlines the very visual strength of her writing.

The fourteen stories that made up *The Rendezvous & Other Stories*, published by Gollancz in 1980, are a perfect example of her range and creativity. The case of the seemingly happily married woman who committed suicide in Paris for no apparent reason; an ambitious author plagued by women whom he has used in his climb up the literary ladder; and a young man, doomed to be a cripple, trying to break the news to the beautiful girl he had hoped to marry. Those are just three of her varied themes. Interestingly some of them were written before her first novel was published.

In another collection *Not After Midnight,* five long short stories, she showed that her settings could be as varied as her plots: Jerusalem and East Anglia, Venice and Ireland.

It was one of the most painful twists of reality in her personal life story that her husband, who liked Kilmarth, died a few weeks after signing the lease, and never lived there. Janet Watts, interviewing her for *The Observer* in 1981, asked her if the passage of time, had made widowhood easier to bear. Then, sixteen years after her husband's death, she confessed, 'I don't know.'

ABOVE: **Joan Fontaine today.**

LEFT: **Joan Fontaine and Daphne du Maurier at their only meeting at Kilmarth in 1967.**

Rule Britannia
THE LAST NOVEL

Daphne du Maurier's final chapter is *Rule Britannia* and it was inspired by her experience of living at Kilmarth. This, her thirteenth novel, revolves around the character of Mad and an 'invasion' of Cornwall by the Americans. Mad is addicted to her home and says she would certainly die for it ' . . . if I thought it would be any good'. One feels very strongly that those are the sentiments of the author too. Moreover Daphne du Maurier understands that Cornwall is almost an island: a fact reflected in her narrative as she justifies the force of Mad's determination to defend

her beloved Cornwall. In this novel US marines land in Cornwall and Mad rallies friends, family and neighbours to protect their heritage.

Emma lives in Cornwall with her grandmother, a distinguished and now retired actress. Mad is Emma's name for her grandmother. The book is in fact dedicated to Gladys Cooper, a long-time friend. Granddaughter and grandmother in the novel wake one morning to find their world shattered: no telephone and no radio, no post and a warship in the bay with American troops advancing across the field in the direction of their home. This fictitious time is when as a nation we have withdrawn from the Common Market and, with the threat of bankruptcy, it has been decided that solution and salvation lies in a union with the United States. In theory it is a partnership, but some perceptive people see it as a takeover bid. From the moment she sees the Americans, Mad declares war of a kind on these interlopers.

This is, in fact, Daphne du Maurier at the height of her powers – perceptive and drawing lifelike characters. Fifteen years on, it is still hard to believe that this was her last novel and nothing can alter that sad fact, but at least, it is a wonderful finale in the true du Maurier tradition. As the jacket blurb reflects: 'In Emma, looking at it all with clear young eyes, Daphne du Maurier has drawn one of her most enchanting heroines; and this engrossing book shows again what a versatile and perceptive writer she is.'

LEFT: There are basically no real place names in 'Rule Britannia', just fleeting references to St Michael's Mount, St Mawgan, Falmouth etc., but in the reader's imagination, especially those who know and understand Cornwall, one can see the setting as St Austell Bay and Par Beach.

HARBOUR OFFICES

Vanishing Cornwall

After this last novel, Daphne du Maurier continued to write, fascinated by the Elizabethan lives of the Bacon Boys which resulted in two more biographies, entitled *The Winding Stairs* and *The Golden Lads.* Of these two books she reflected: 'What interested me most when doing my Bacon research, I found that the maternal grandmother of Anthony and Frances Bacon had been Ann FitzWilliam of Milton, near Peterborough, daughter of Sir William Fitzwilliam, friend of Wolsey and the first to live at Milton.' Neither of these books achieved great success and the author sadly reflected: 'The trouble is I'm afraid the public see me essentially as a novelist and not a biographer.'

On the subject of her own reading habits, Daphne has always insisted, 'I never reopen my own work. Once it is finished that is it, I just put it away.'

In the early '80s Daphne du Maurier's book *Vanishing Cornwall* was reissued with colour photographs and the original text — the photographs being taken by her son Christian Browning. In a way it is her tribute to Cornwall containing chapters on the search of Arthur and of Tristan, the High Coast and The Lizard, religion and superstition. Writing the original version at Menabilly in 1966 she dedicated it: 'To the memory of my husband because of memories shared and a mutual love of Cornwall; and to our son Christian, who photographed the present while I rambled on about the past.'

In the words of Tamsin Mitchell on Radio Cornwall in 1987, this 'will stand as a lasting tribute to one woman's love of Cornwall for many years to come'.

More than twenty years after publication, it remains a fine volume — as vivid and readable as any of her thirteen novels. In fact, the reality in places, is so colourful and dramatic that one is reminded of the truth of an ancient cliché — that fact is truly stranger than fiction.

In looking at the life and times of this distinguished novelist one is tempted to ask, or at least, wonder: 'How much fiction is drawn from the well of personal experience and emotion?'

She confessed there were always two lives to Daphne du Maurier: her marriage and the bringing up of two daughters and a son, and her writing self imagining someone else's life.'

BELOW: The River Fowey in its early stages and, on the preceding spread, when it reaches the town of Fowey. This lovely Cornish river, which begins just below Brown Willy on Bodmin Moor, flows down to Golitha Falls, past Lanhydrock, Restormel, Lostwithiel to where it meets the sea beyond Fowey and Polruan. Fowey River has played a most vital role in the Cornish life of Daphne du Maurier. She has sailed on it and written about it with affection and understanding. She has understood the significance of its history and its part in shaping the character and destiny of this corner of Cornwall. It is hard to believe this small ribbon of water will, miles on, become the majestic river used by large vessels – a water way which has played a big part in this history and legends of Cornwall.

Dame Daphne at 80

'A hired car swept around the curve of the hill and suddenly the full expanse of Fowey Harbour was spread beneath us. The contrast of this sheet of white water, the nearby jetties, the moored ships, the grey roofs of Fowey across the way, the clustering cottages of Polruan on the opposite hill by the harbour mouth and narrow claustrophobic Looe where we had spent the night was astonishing. Like a gateway to another world. My spirits soared.'

That is how Dame Daphne opened a radio programme celebrating her eightieth birthday in 1987 produced by Tamsin Mitchell on Radio Cornwall. In that same programme her son Christian said: 'She's always written about places more than necessarily the people and obviously different places in Cornwall when she first went there as a child, and they had Ferryside as a holiday home in Fowey. The whole atmosphere affected her . . . if it wasn't Cornwall it would have been Brittany in France or the west coast of Scotland, somewhere wild, somewhere that has legends, mysteries. I don't think she would have written or found somewhere like Essex particularly invigorating or having the same sort of mystery that Cornwall has. *The Loving Spirit,* her first novel which came out in 1931, was all written closely around Fowey . . . of a family . . . of generations in a different family and seeing them through. *Jamaica Inn, Frenchman's Creek, The King's General, The House on the Strand* in more recent times, again all set in and around Cornwall having Cornwall as really the setting for each of those. So I think it's very much a part of her writing.'

In the words of the programme: 'If Ferryside captured Daphne du Maurier's heart, then Menabilly just outside Fowey captured her total being. When she moved there, she used the house and the surrounding

Dame Daphne said of her present home: 'I'm equally content here at Kilmarth.' On her eightieth birthday she told the author: 'When I first stopped writing I did find it difficult to relax because I had no hobbies – writing has always been my one and only interest. But today I am accustomed to not writing, and I do feel well even at eighty.'

area to great effect in her books. Ten years earlier on that long-running BBC radio programme, *Desert Island Discs,* she explained to Roy Plomley how she first came.

'Well there were my trespassing days, we walked a lot my sisters and I and we used to trespass around the grounds of Menabilly just the other side of the harbour from us at Fowey . . . this house wasn't lived in because the owner lived away — he used to come down sometimes — and I got a terrific thing about this house, and eventually many years afterwards came to live there. I asked if I could possibly rent it during the war, and went to live there . . . with the children, my husband was off in the war, from '43 till after he died in 1965.'

Later in the programme she admitted with enthusiasm: 'Oh, I have a terrific thing about the past.' Then there was reference to Sir Arthur Quiller-Couch giving his inaugural lecture at Cambridge University: 'His words could almost have been used to sum up Daphne du Maurier's skill:

The beauty and the mystery beckon still.

"Literature isn't an abstract science to which exact definitions can be applied. It's an art, the success of which depends upon personal persuasiveness . . . "'

She concluded her eightieth birthday programme with these words, 'When I wrote *Vanishing Cornwall* I lived at Menabilly, a happy tenant. Now I'm equally content at Kilmarth' — and of the beloved Cornwall: 'The beauty and the mystery beckon still.'

Daphne du Maurier is a caster of spells.

That fact is confirmed in a truly beautiful book which celebrated her 80th birthday. *Classics of the Macabre,* published by Victor Gollancz, is a sumptuous volume, brilliantly, imaginatively illustrated in glowing colour by Michael Foreman.

In her Note to the Reader, Dame Daphne tells us how her stories have often started – something or someone who has caught her eagle eye.

It is a surprise therefore to learn she is not psychic and has never seen a ghost 'or dabbled in spiritualism or the occult.' Nevertheless she admits: 'I have always been fascinated by the unexplained, the darker side of life. I have a strong sense of the things that lie *beyond* our day-by-day perception and experience. It is, perhaps, an extension of this feeling that makes me live through the characters that I create.'

Dame Daphne is undeniably an artist. She can 'paint' tellingly, as effectively as any painter. In the eye of her imagination, *we are there.*

She is a writer for all seasons.

Other Bossiney Titles Include

FOWEY – RIVER AND TOWN
by Sarah Foot
An enlarged and updated edition of 'Following the River Fowey'.
'Sarah Foot has a passion for Cornish rivers . . . traces the Fowey from its beginning just below Brown Willy on Bodmin Moor down to where it meets the sea beyond Fowey and Polruan.'
Cornish Scene

'The intricate tapestries of this delightful area are woven together with understanding interviews . . . buy, beg or borrow it.'
The Cornish Times

PEOPLE AND PLACES IN CORNWALL
by Michael Williams
Featuring Sir John Betjeman, Marika Hanbury Tenison, Barbara Hepworth and seven other characters, all of whom contributed richly to the Cornish scene.
'. . . outlines ten notable characters . . . whose lives and work have been influenced by "Cornwall's genius to fire creativity" . . . a fascinating study.'
The Cornish Guardian

E.V. THOMPSON'S WESTCOUNTRY
This is a memorable journey: a combination of colour and black-and-white photography. Bristol to Land's End happens to be the Bossiney region, and this is precisely E.V. Thompson's Westcountry.
'Stunning photographs and fascinating facts make this an ideal book for South West tourists and residents alike – beautifully atmospheric colour shots make browsing through the pages a real delight.'
Jane Leigh, Express & Echo

COASTLINE OF CORNWALL
by Ken Duxbury
Ken Duxbury has spent thirty years sailing the seas of Cornwall, walking its clifftops, exploring its caves and beaches, using its harbours and creeks.
'. . . a trip in words and pictures from Hawker's Morwenstow in the north, round Land's End and the Lizard to the gentle slopes of Mount Edgcumbe country park.'
The Western Morning News

FESTIVALS OF CORNWALL
by Douglas Williams
Douglas Williams explores some of the great Cornish occasions in the calendar: Hurling and Gorsedd, Crying the Neck and Marhamchurch Revel, Flora Day at Helston and Obby Oss at Padstow are only some of the events covered in words and photographs.
'Douglas Williams has come up trumps again . . . captures the individual character of the county's festivals through his love of Cornwall and all things Cornish.'
The Cornishman

MY CORNWALL
A personal vision of this Celtic land by eleven writers: Daphne du Maurier, Ronald Duncan, James Turner, Angela du Maurier, Jack Clemo, Denys Val Baker, Colin Wilson, C.C. Vyvyan, Arthur Caddick, Michael Williams and Derek Tangye with reproductions of paintings by Margo Maeckelberghe and splendid black and white photographs.
'. . . gives a valuable insight into the many facets of this fascinating land . . . '
John Marquis, The Falmouth Packet

THE MOORS OF CORNWALL
by Michael Williams
Contains 77 photographs and drawings.
The first ever publication to incorporate the three main moorland areas of Cornwall.
'. . . is not only a celebration in words of the moors and their ancient pagan stones and granite strewn tors but a remarkable collection of photographs and drawings of Penwith, Goss and Bodmin Moors . . . '
Sarah Foot, The Editor, Cornish Scene

We shall be pleased to send you our catalogue giving full details of our growing list of titles for Devon, Cornwall and Somerset as well as other forthcoming publications.

If you have difficulty in obtaining our titles, write direct to Bossiney Books, Land's End, St Teath, Bodmin, Cornwall.
